The monkeys and
apes brought together
in this book come from
many different countries
all over the world.

For Cooper
P. H.

For all the monkeys at Twycross Zoo,
including Janet, Malcolm and Betty
P. C.

Text copyright © 1993 by Peter Hansard
Illustrations copyright © 1993 by Patricia Casey

First U.S. edition 1993

Published in Great Britain in 1993 by Walker Books Ltd., London.
Library of Congress Cataloging-in-Publication Data

Hansard, Peter.
I like monkeys because— / Peter Hansard ; illustrated by Patricia Casey.—
1st U.S. ed.
p. cm. — (Read and wonder books)
Summary: Describes a variety of monkeys and apes around the world
and some of the interesting things they do.
ISBN 1-56402-196-3
1. Monkeys—Juvenile literature. 2. Primates—Juvenile literature.
[1. Monkeys. 2. Apes.] I.Casey, Patricia, ill. II. Title. III. Series: Read and wonder.
QL737.P9H243   1993
599.8—dc20   92-54409

10 9 8 7 6 5 4 3 2 1

Printed in Hong Kong

The pictures in this book were done in pencil and watercolor.

Candlewick Press
2067 Massachusetts Avenue
Cambridge, Massachusetts 02140

I LIKE MONKEYS BECAUSE...

Peter Hansard

illustrated by Patricia Casey

CANDLEWICK PRESS

CAMBRIDGE, MASSACHUSETTS

Spider monkeys

When the sun comes up,
it's hungry monkey time.
Time to look for fruit and leaves.
Time for breakfast on a branch.

I like monkeys because...
I like the way they huddle.
I like the way they cuddle.

These are spectacled langurs. They have bright orange babies.

I like the way they clean each other's fur.

Hanuman monkeys like these are sacred in India.

I like monkeys because…
I like the funny way they play.
Young ones tease and trick, then
scamper off as fast as they can go.

I like monkeys because…
I like the way they jump
from branch to branch,
from tree to tree.

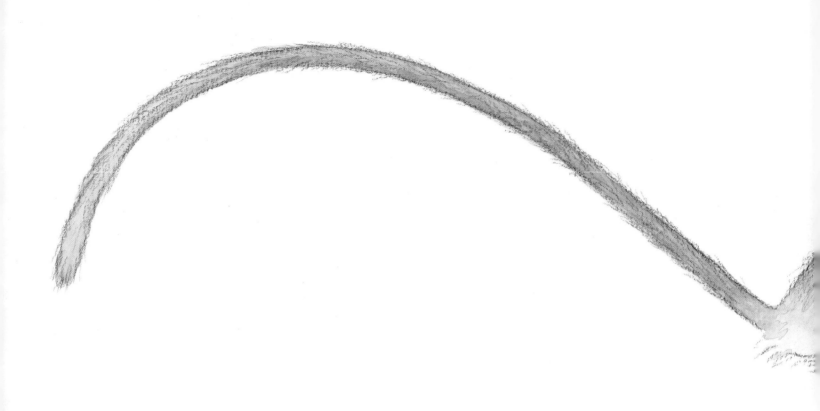

What a mighty leap!

Some
monkeys'
tails
are
longer
than
their
bodies.

Black-and-white colobus

Red-eared guenon

Diana monkey

Mona monkey

Some monkeys talk by making faces.
They flash their eyebrows
and waggle their tongues.
I wonder what they're
saying?

A monkey's paw
is a little hand
with tiny fingernails.

I like baby monkeys because...
they scream and
rush around and
leap and scold
and shriek and
wave their arms
and pull and tug

and cause
all sorts
of problems.

Mother carries baby
tucked up underneath
or riding piggyback.
Baby knows to
hang on tight.

Rhesus monkeys are tough and adaptable.
They've even been sent into space.

A black-and-white colobus is often hard to spot in a tree. Its fur looks like hanging moss.

This monkey is beautiful and black-and-white and hairy.

This monkey has a bald head.

Uakari

These monkeys
have long
noses.

male proboscis monkey

female proboscis monkey

When the sun is high,
it's lazy monkey time.
Time to have some lunch.
Time to stretch and yawn.
Time to groom and chatter.

These are tiny squirrel monkeys.

These are big baboons.

Japanese macaques like to bathe in warm water. They wash their potatoes in it, too.

These monkeys keep nice and warm in their volcanic pool. Can you think of a better way to spend a snowy afternoon?

"Orangutan" means "man of the forest" in Malay.

These young apes think
the rain is just a pain.

Orangutans don't like water.

This gorilla is the biggest ape of all.

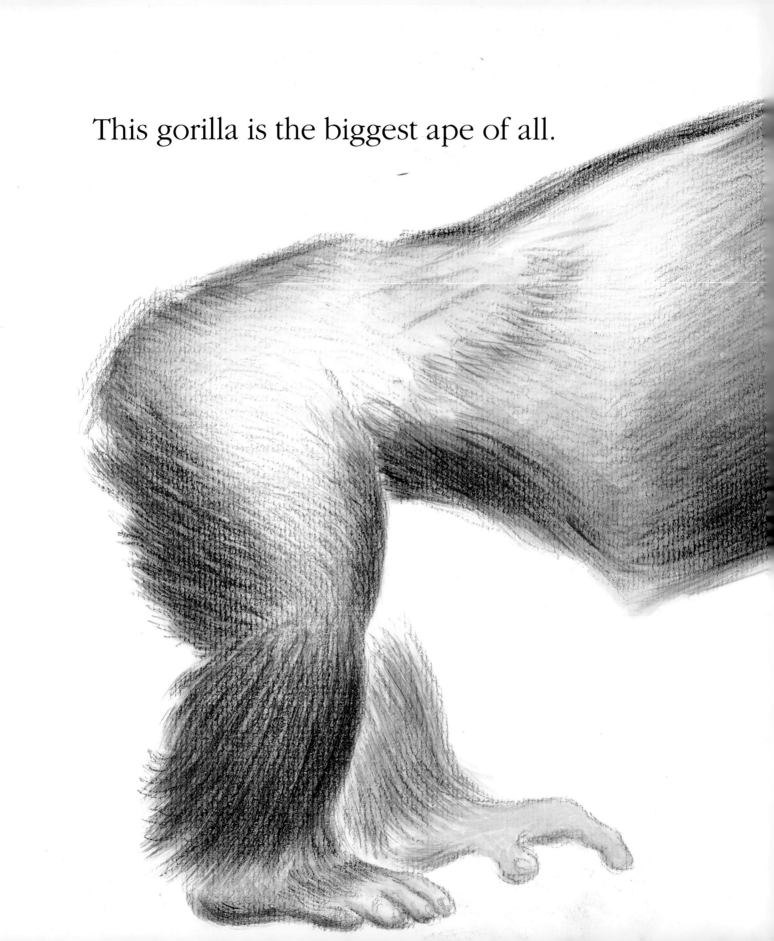

Gorillas are especially gentle.

When the sun is setting,
it's time to settle down.
Time to make a nest of leaves.
Time to cuddle up and snooze.

These apes are chimpanzees. They always sleep in the treetops.